Acknowledgments

First I would like to thank you for purchasing the sneak peek of our first adult coloring book series. Full Blooded Warrior has been a work in progress for the past nine years. This has been a long and tough journey. I would like to thank everybody that supported me along the way. Mama, LeVarr, Derek, Richard, Deasia, Kyle, Corey, Woodrow, J Hoov, Curtis, Christina, Stephanie, Shane & Bacon Gaming, Lakendra, Lenny, Demon eyes Koy, Nayla, & Tria. I have to give a special shoutout to my illustrator Grim and my wonderful wife Derrienne. None of this would be possible without you. In this book we will introduce some of our warriors in the series. Thank you again and enjoy. Checkout our merchandise at http://www.fullbloodedwarrior.com

Facebook:
Full Blooded Warrior

Instagram:
Full Blooded Warrior

Tumblr:
Full Blooded Warrior

Snapchat:
FBWdetroit

FULL-BLOODED WARRIOR

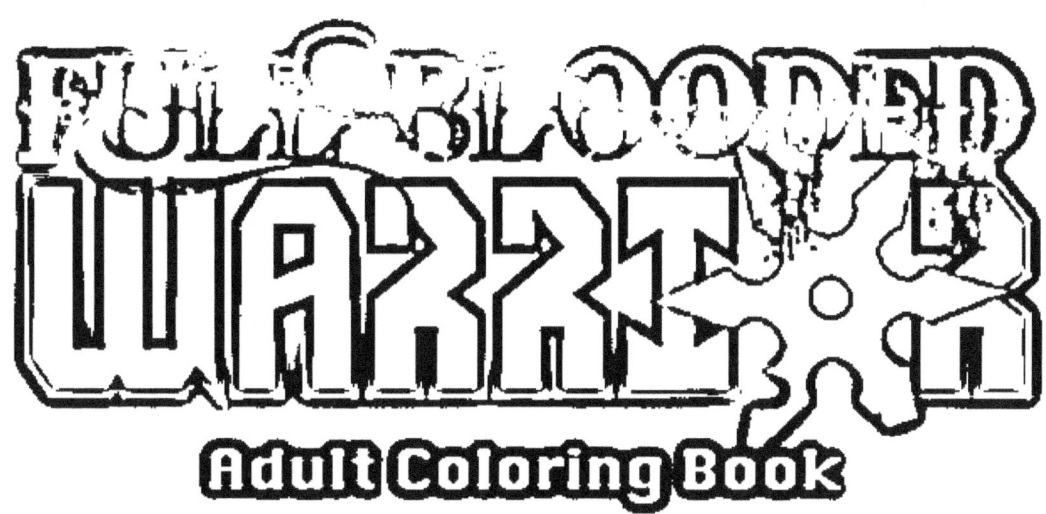

Adult Coloring Book

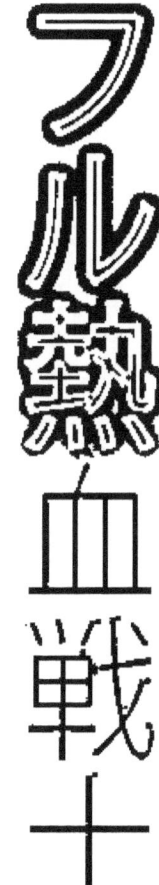

Created BY P.Patton

Artwork BY Grim

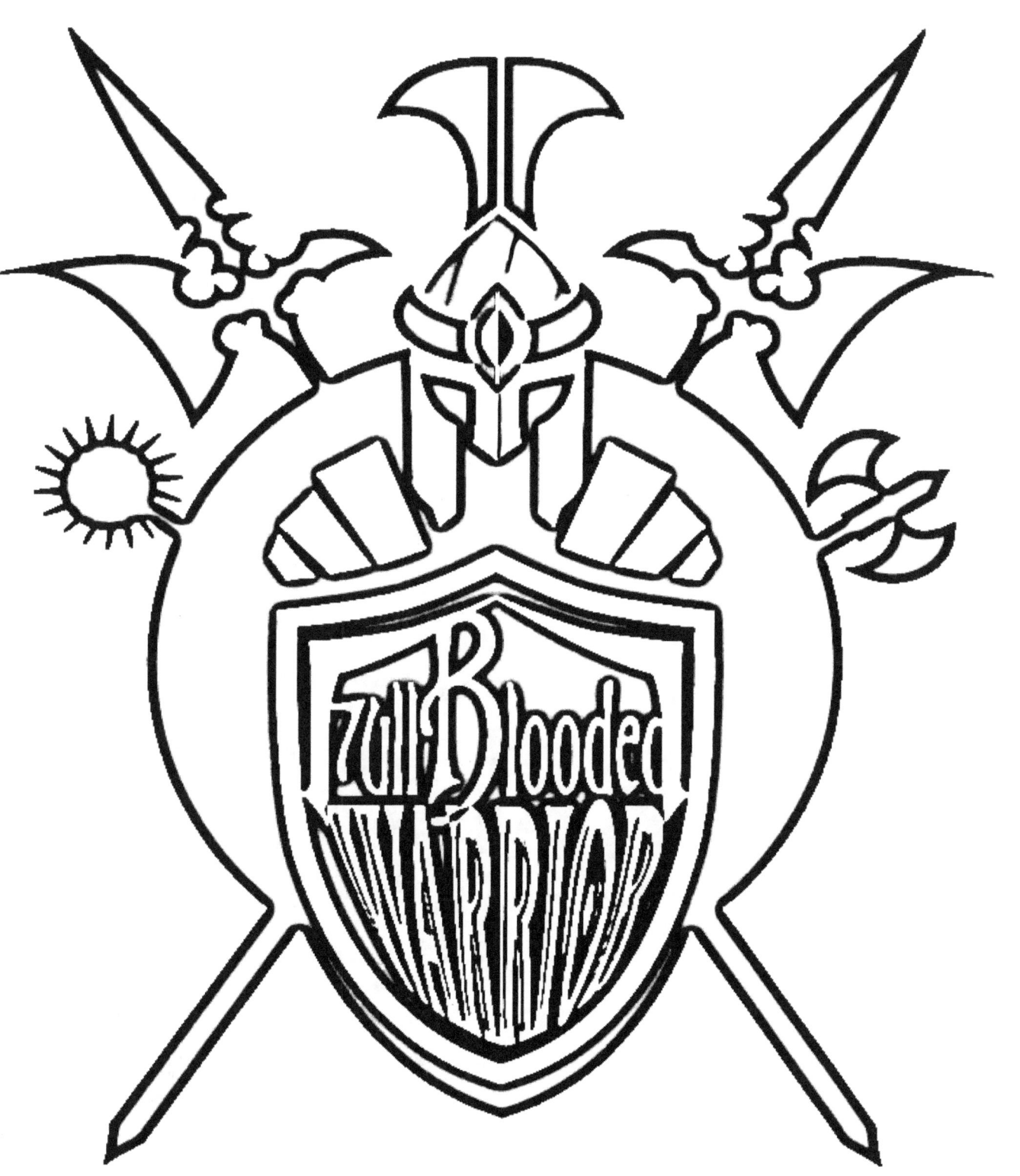

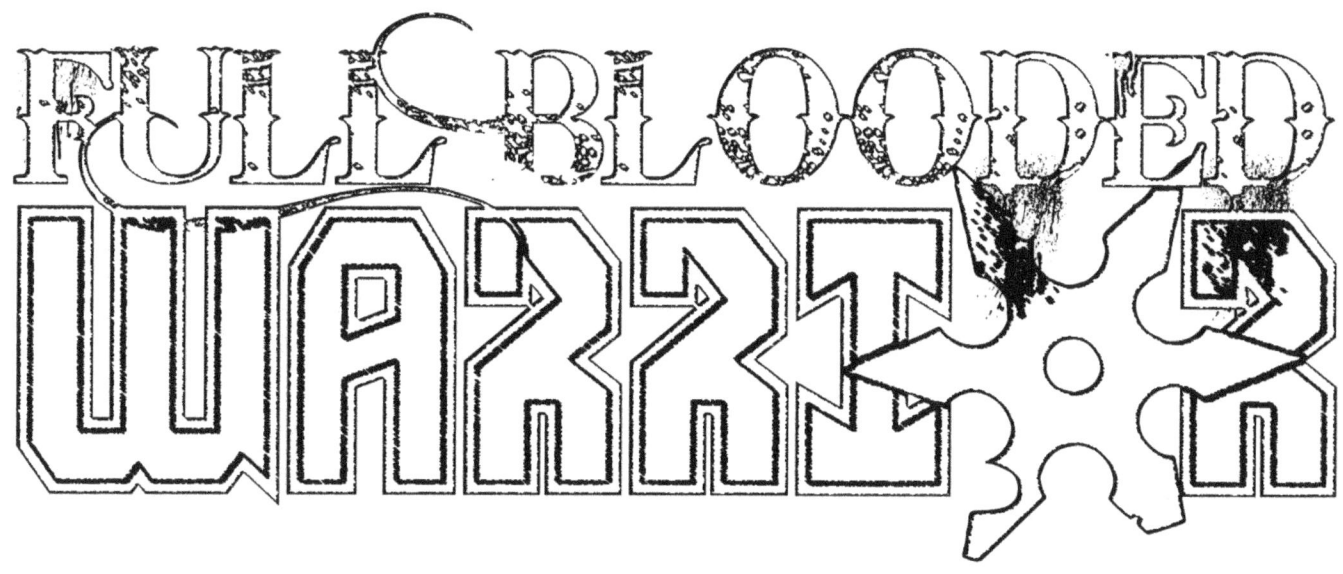

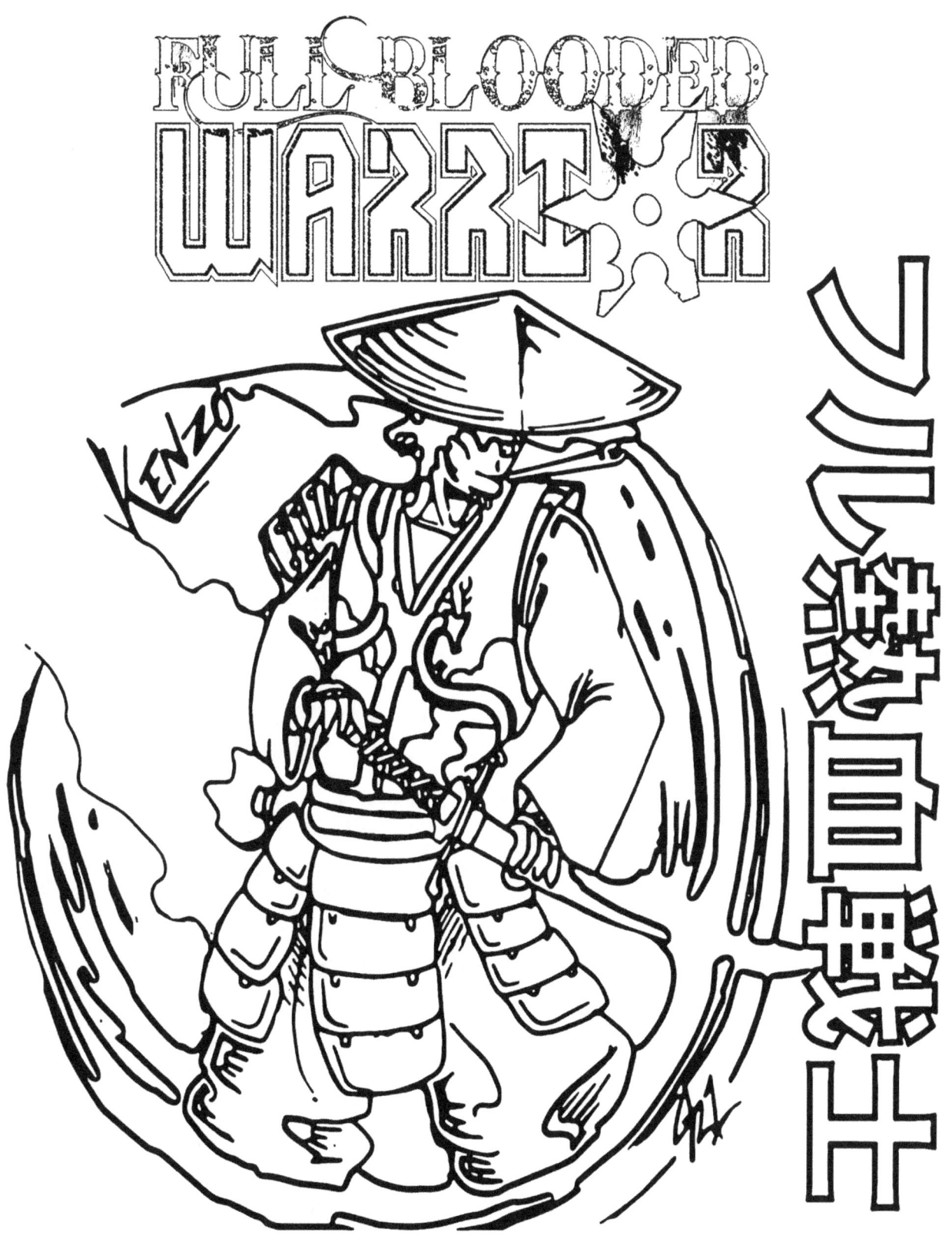

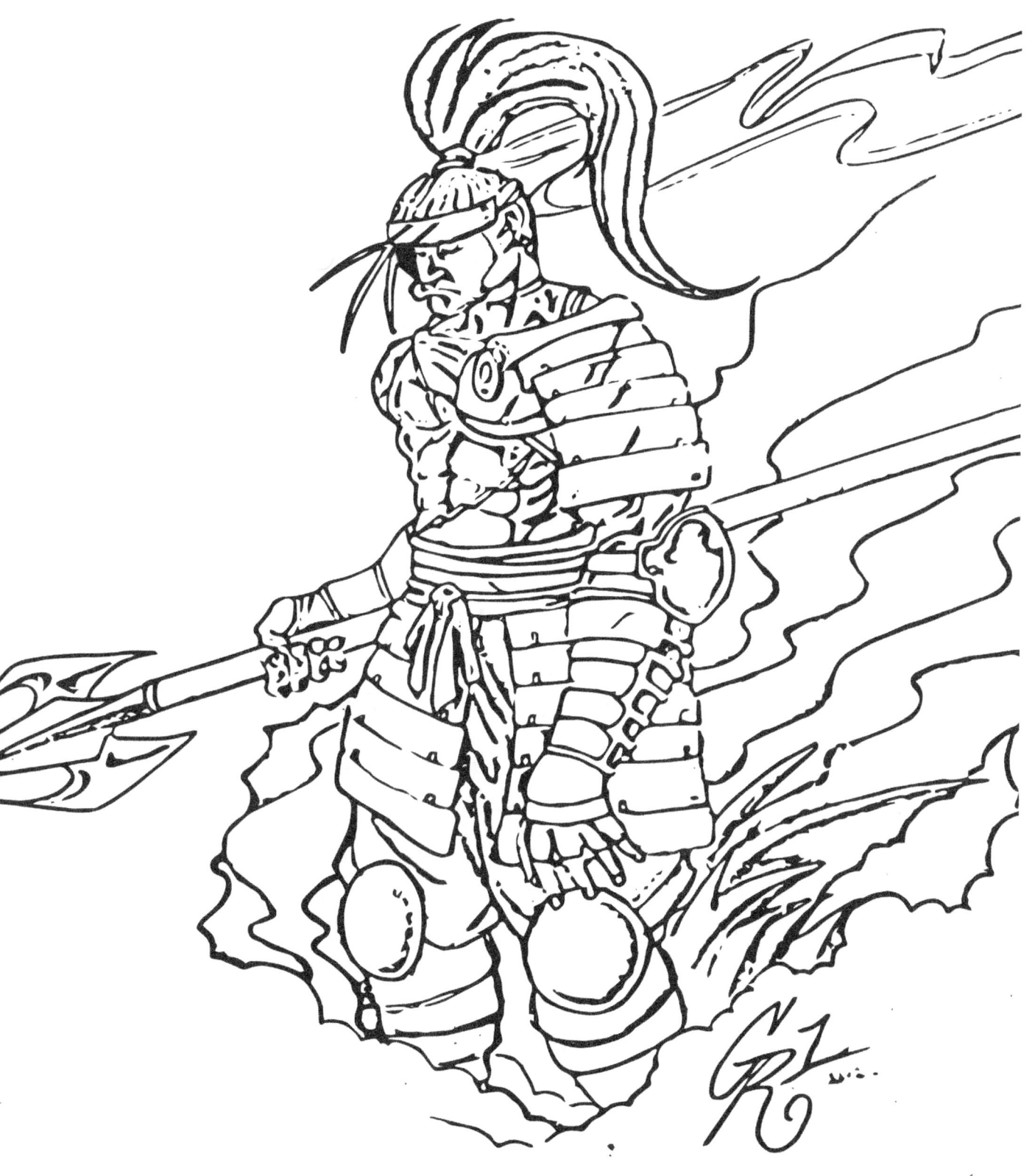

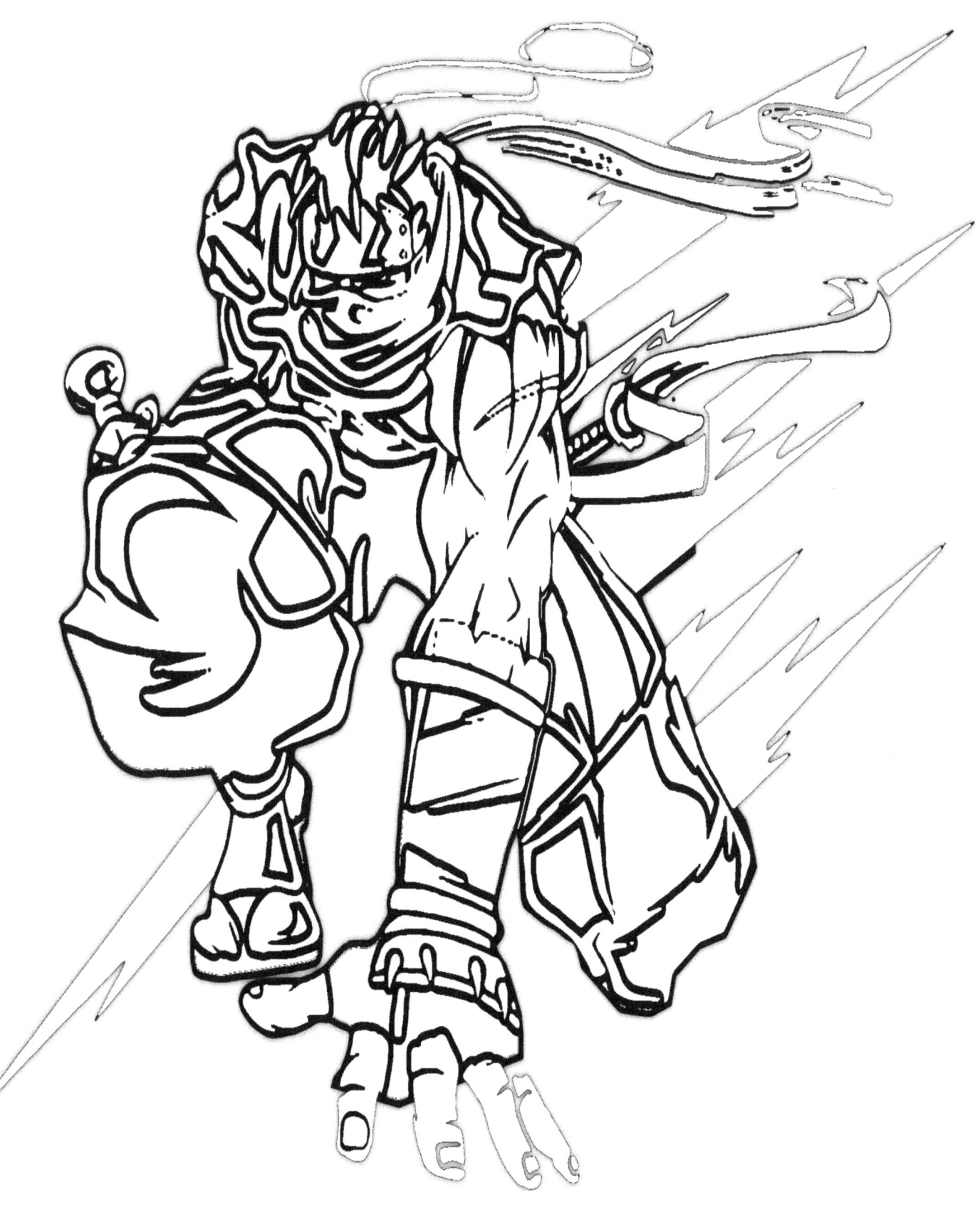

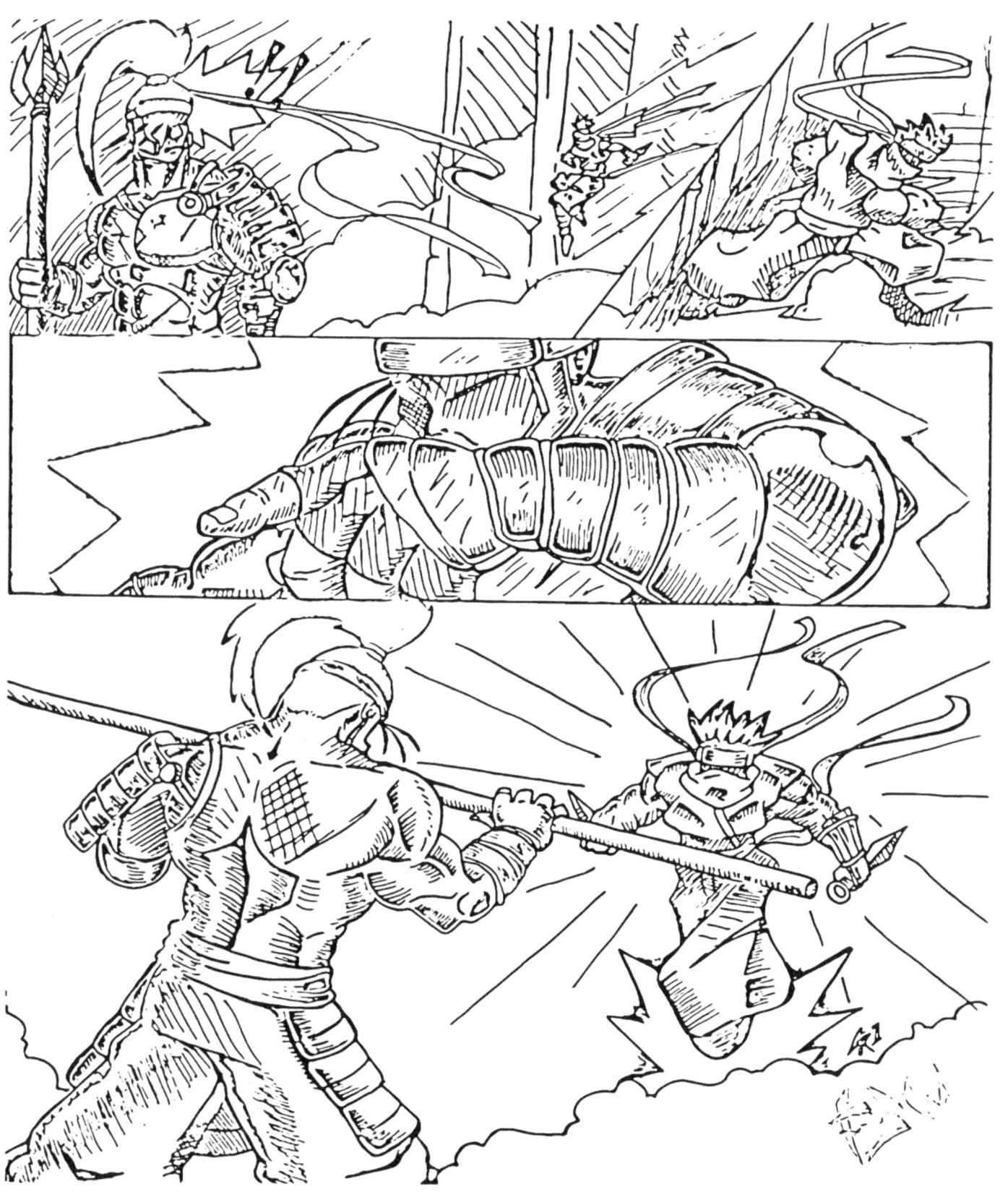

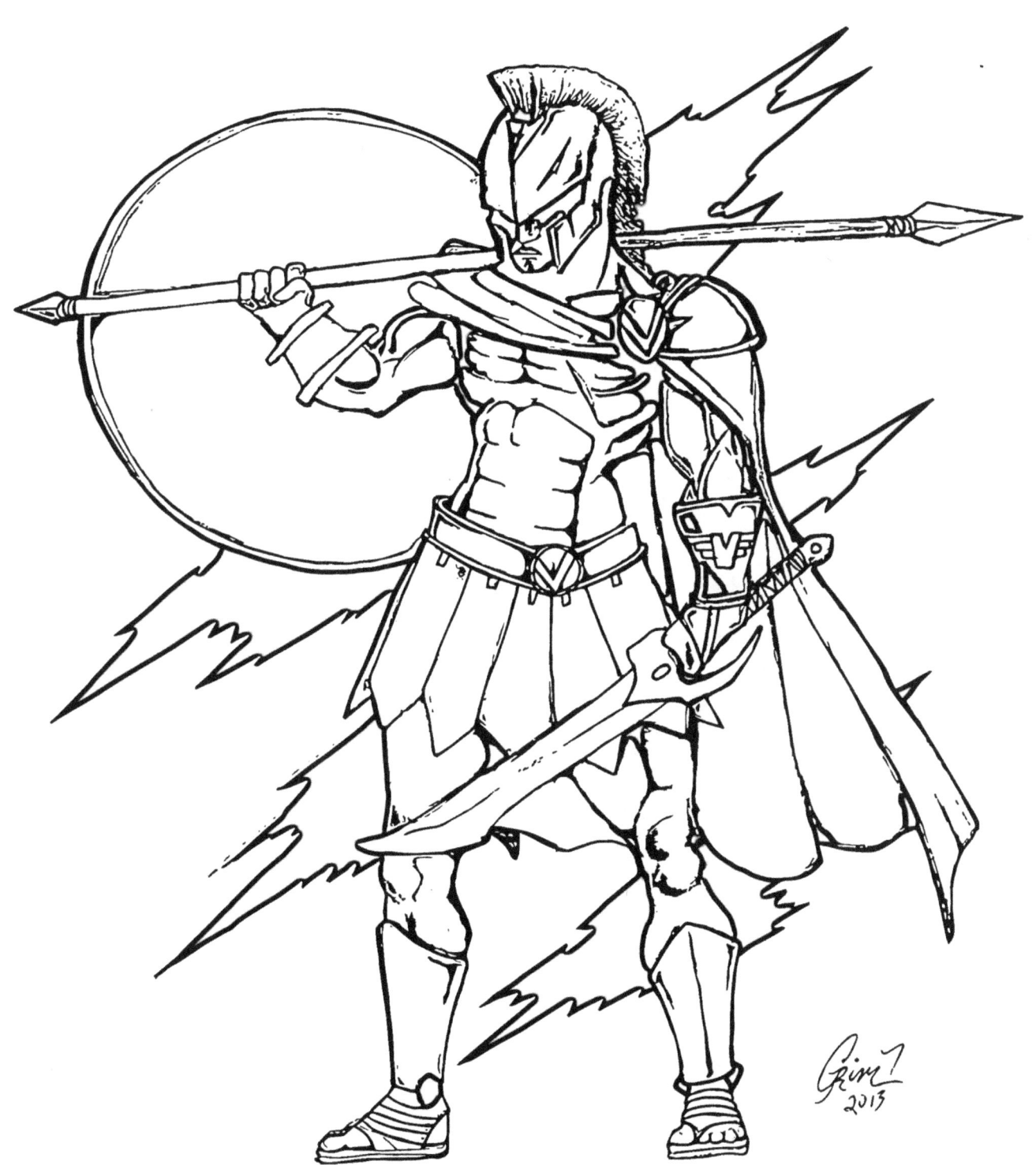

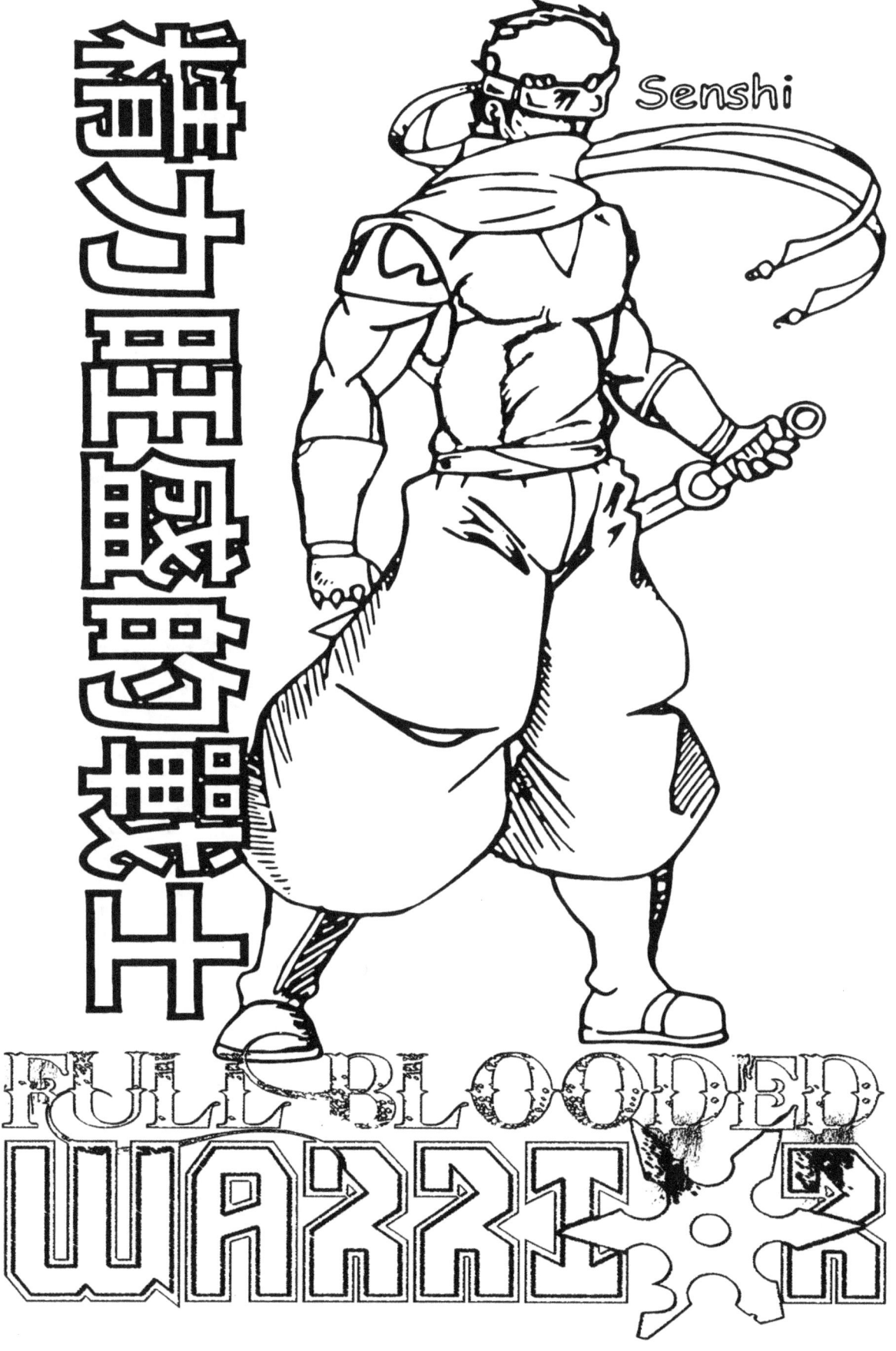

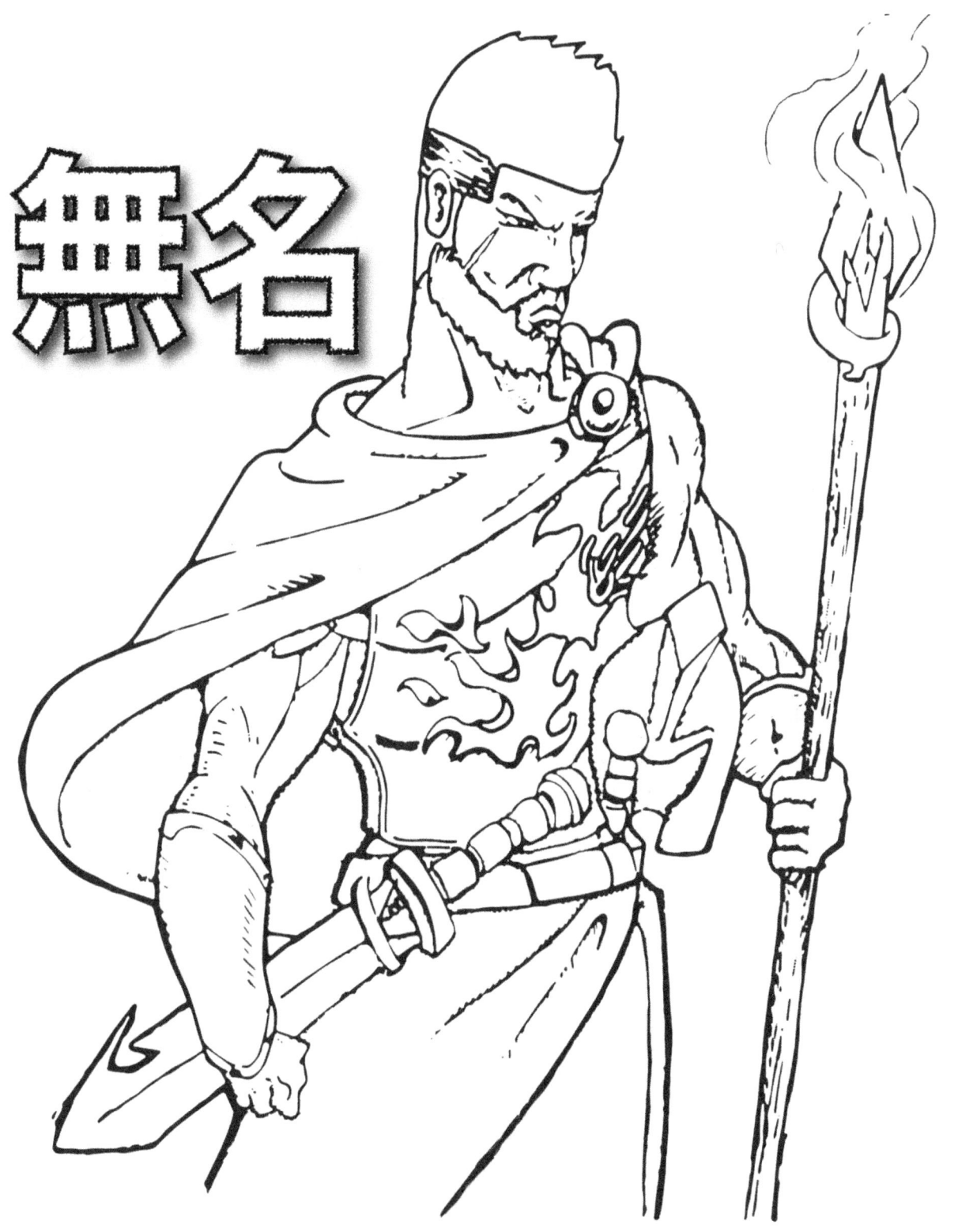

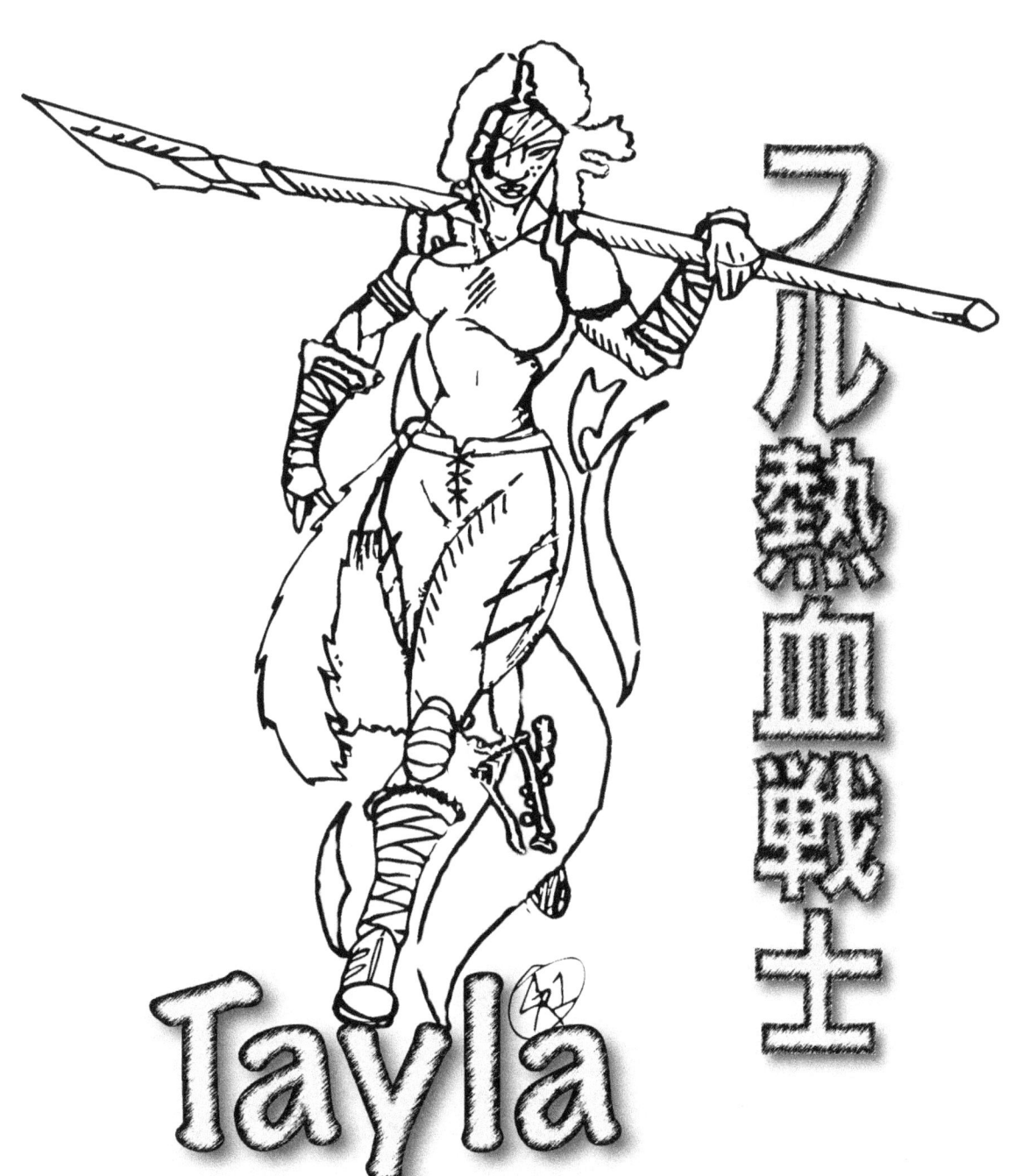
フル熱血戦士

Tayla

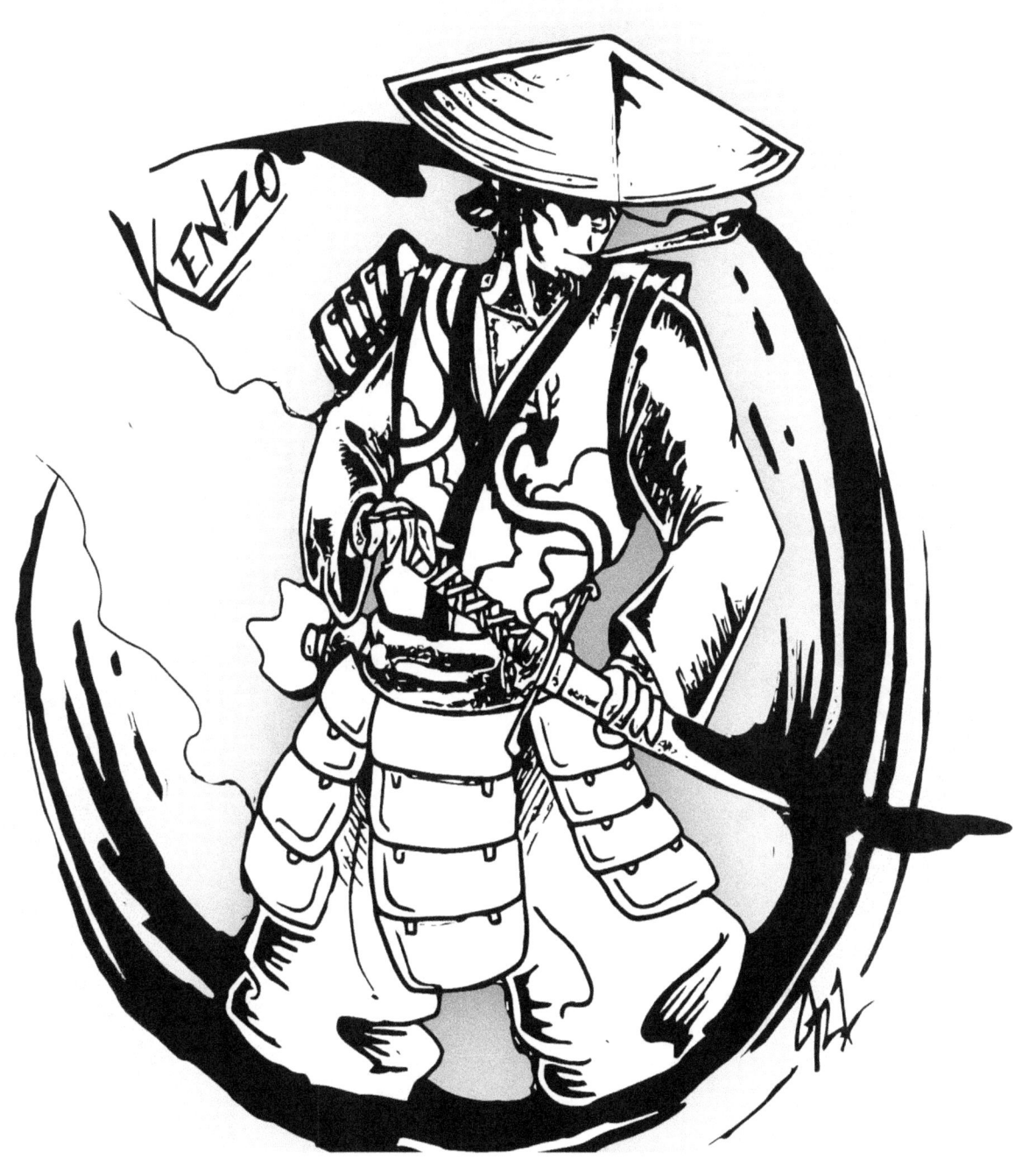

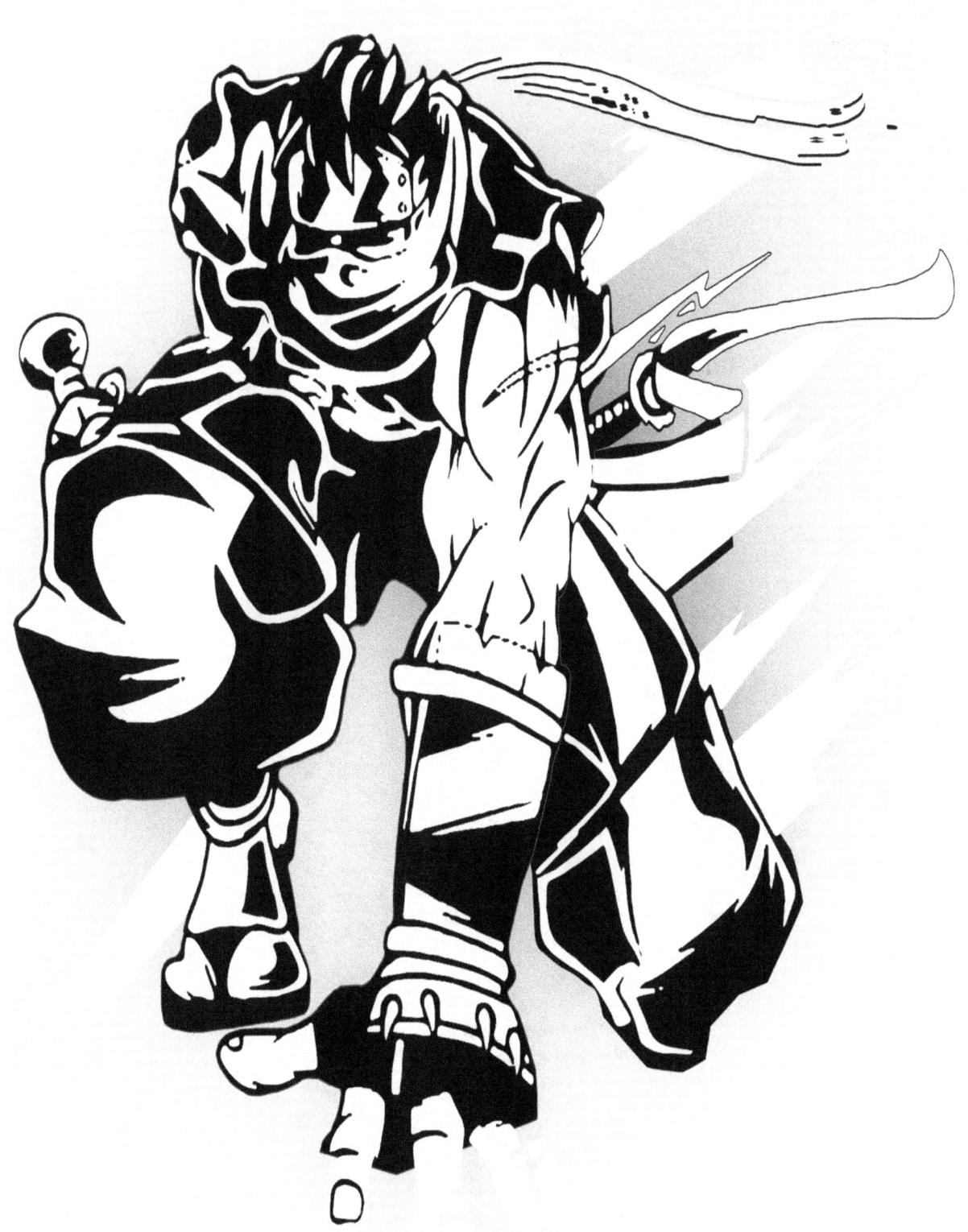

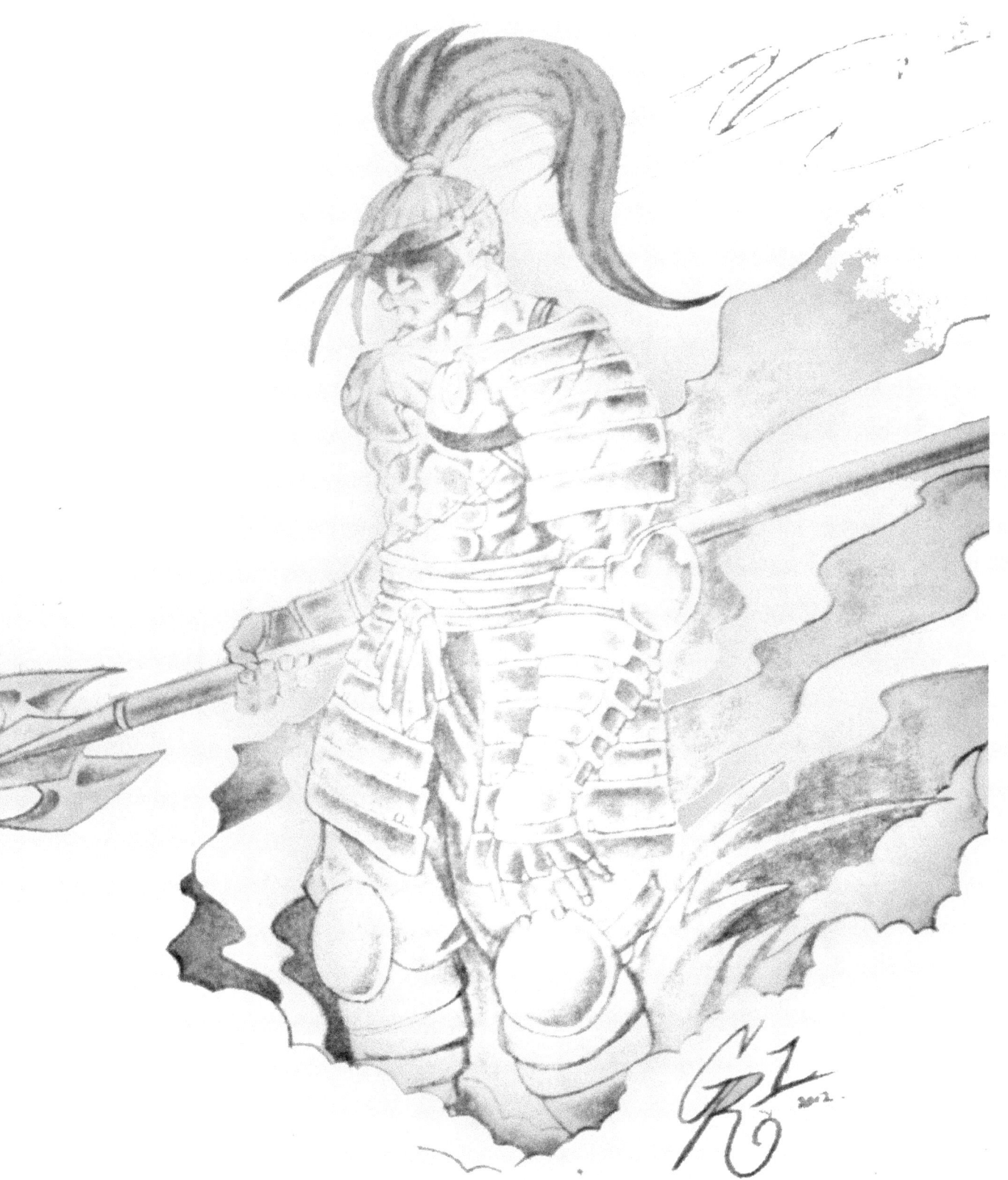

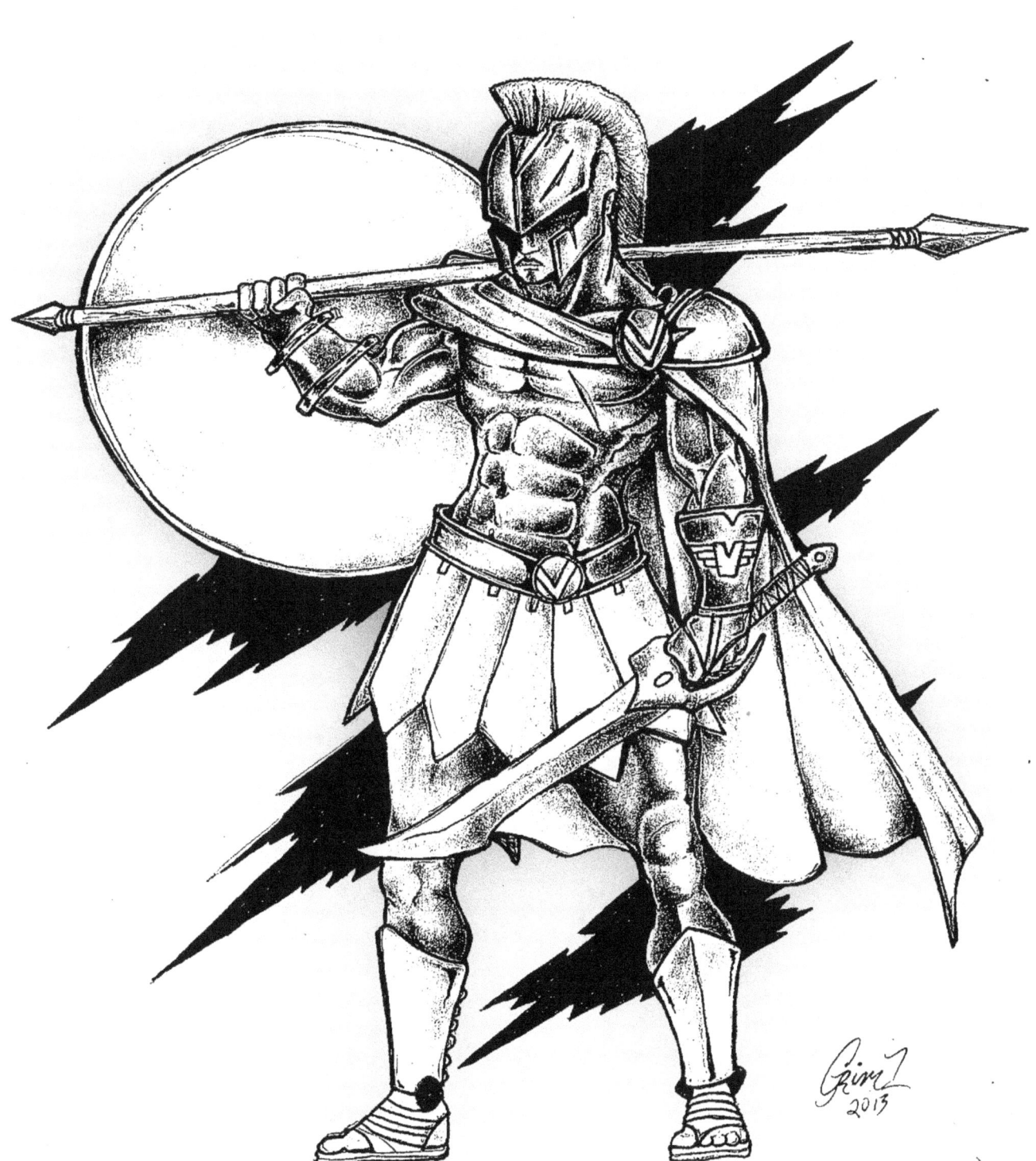

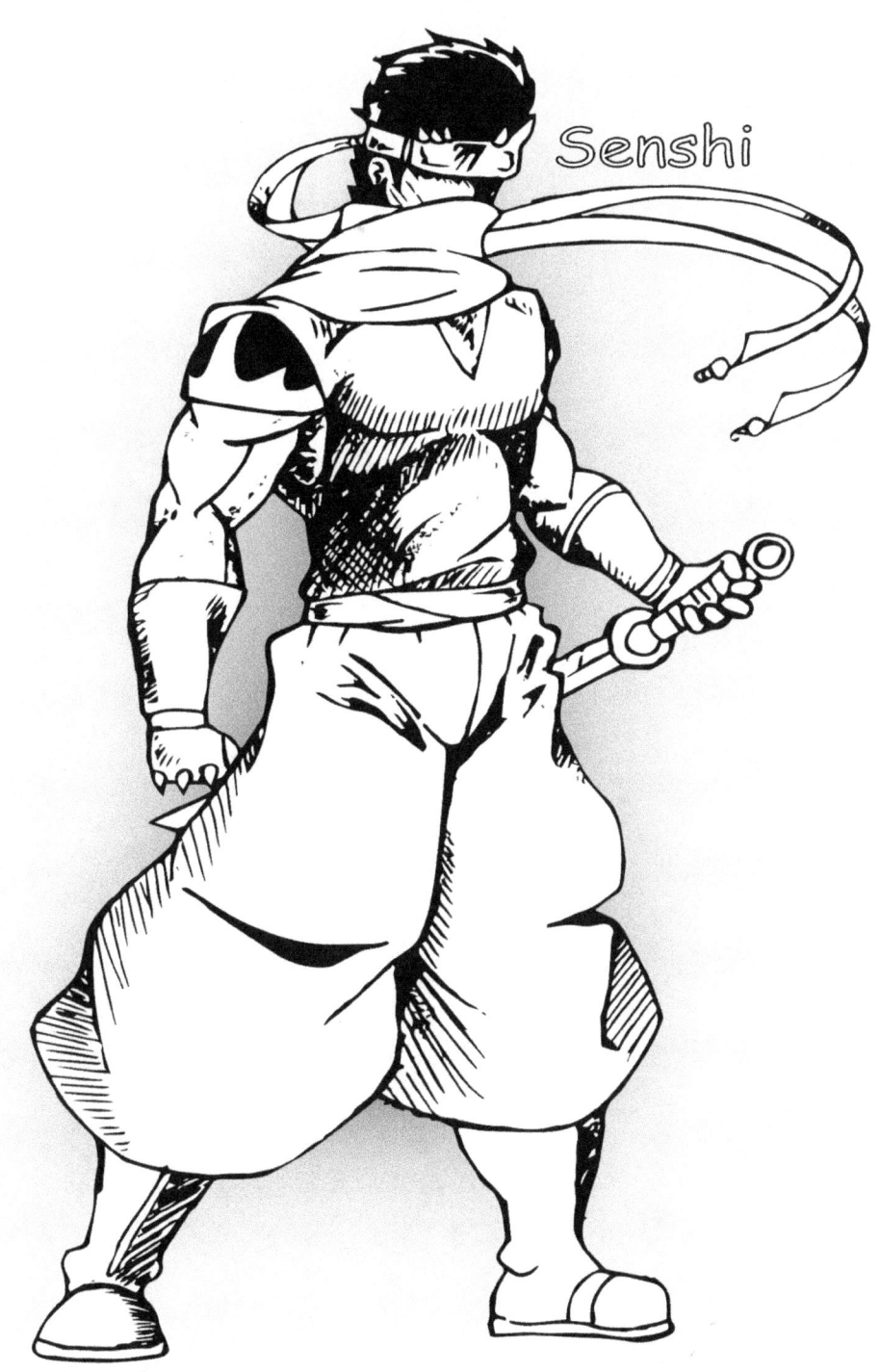

Senshi

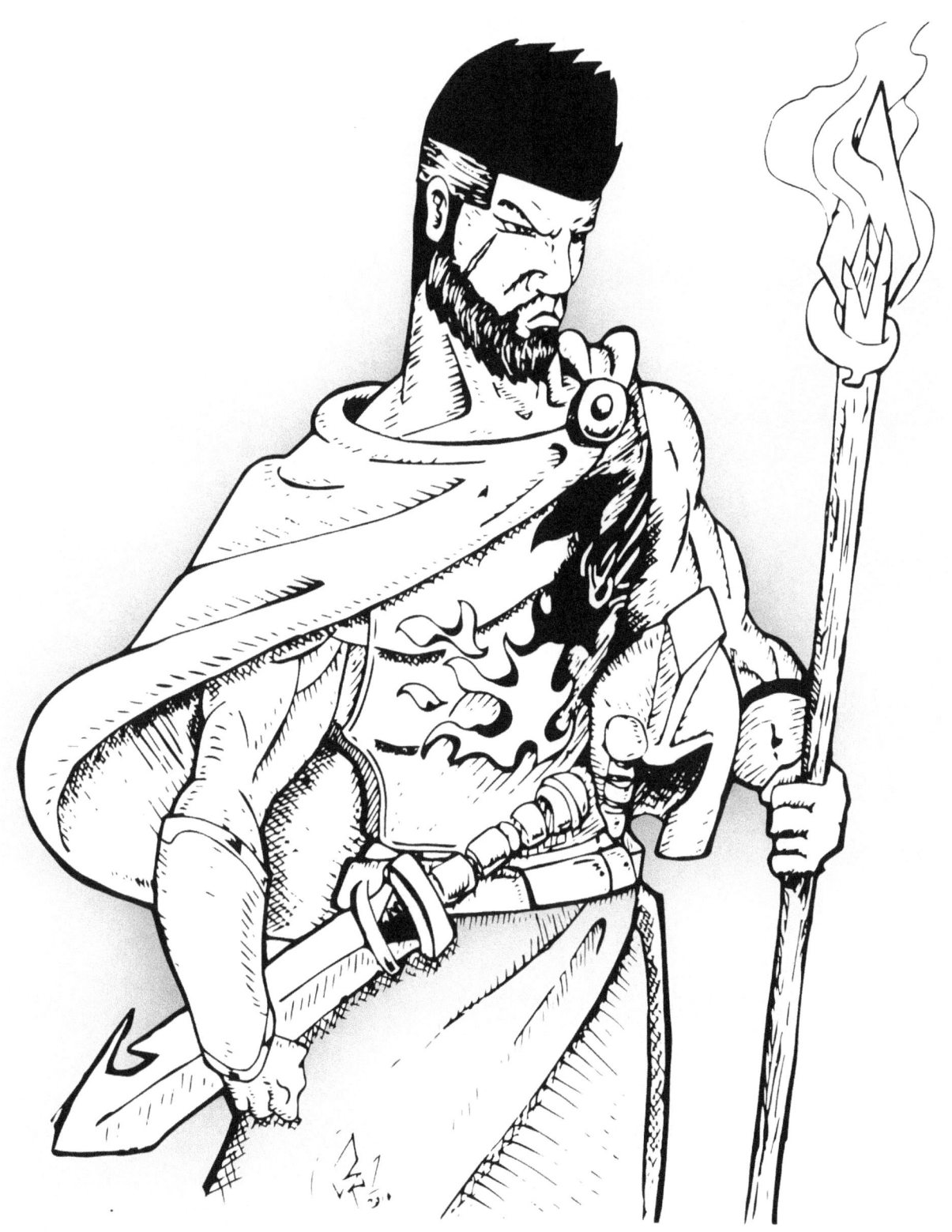

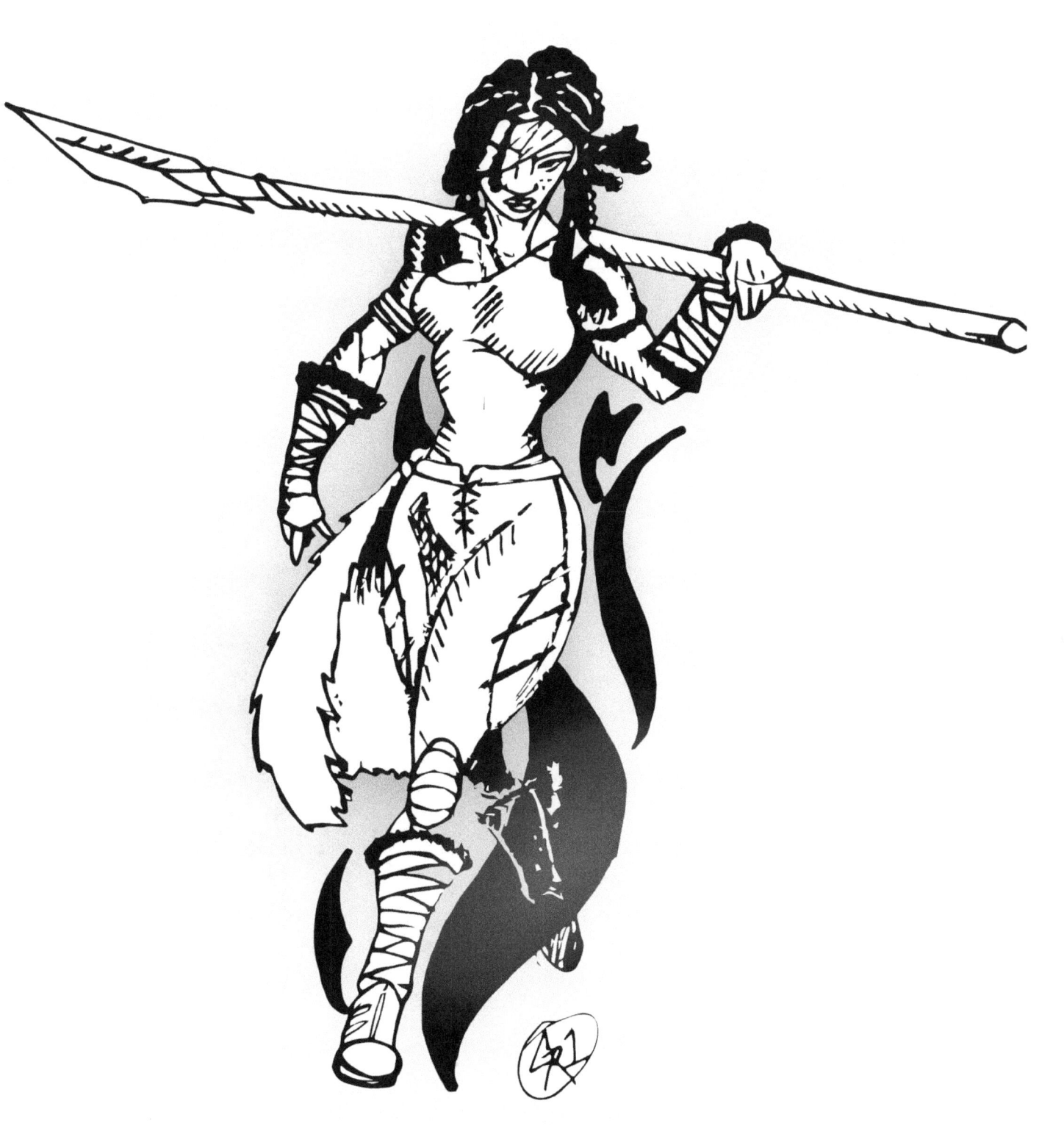

THANK YOU FOR YOUR SUPPORT!

Want to hear about upcoming books, merch, and free pages?

Subscribe to us @ www.fullbloodedwarrior.com/newsletter.

Now a preview of our new series

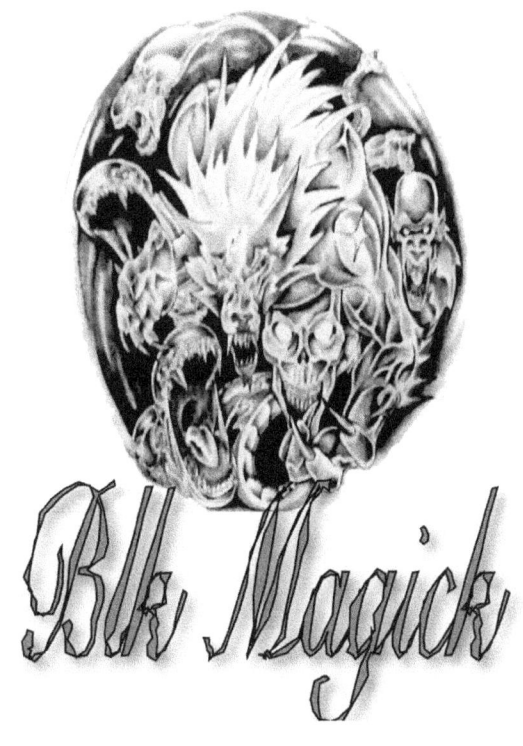

Blk Magick

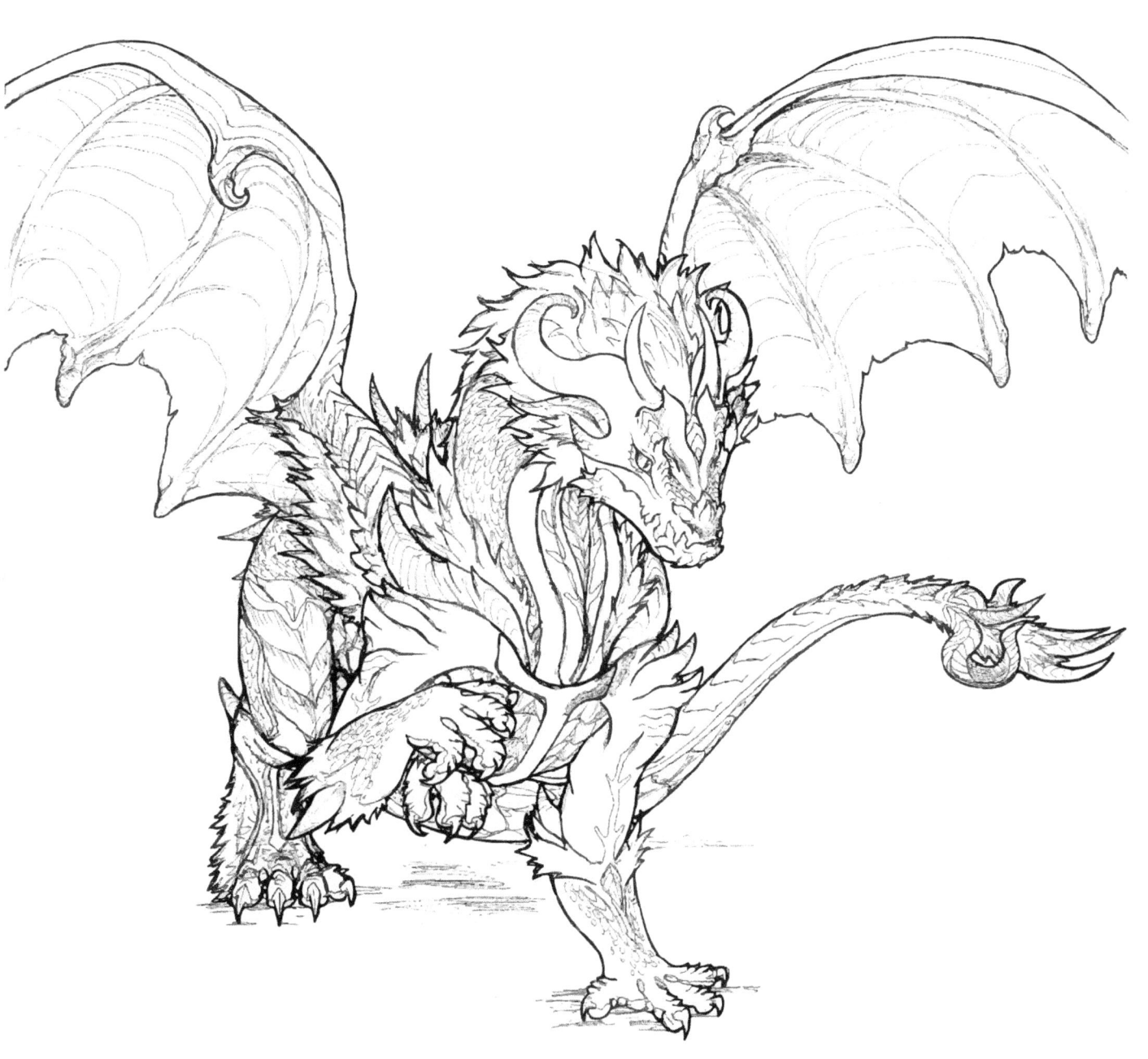

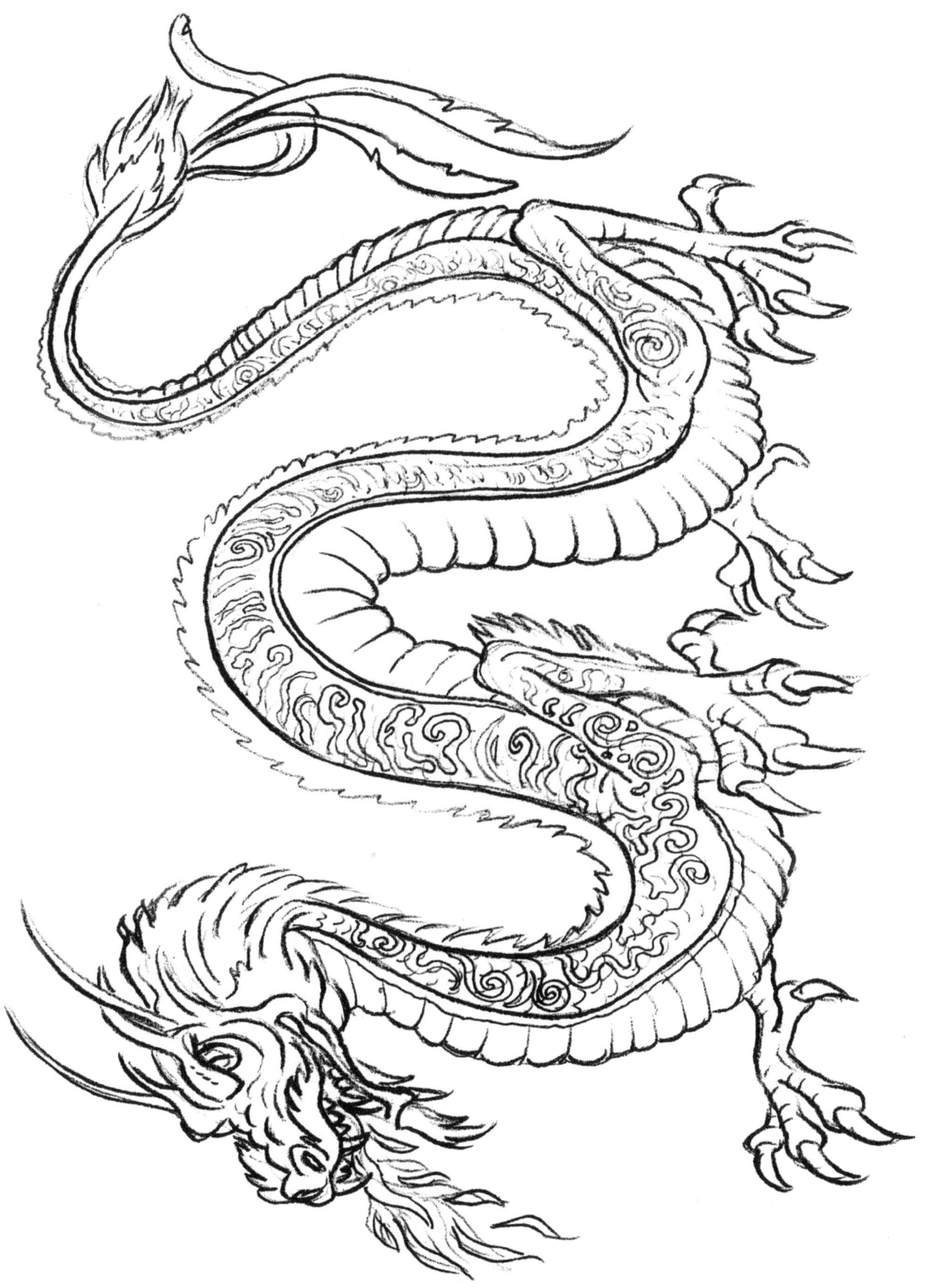

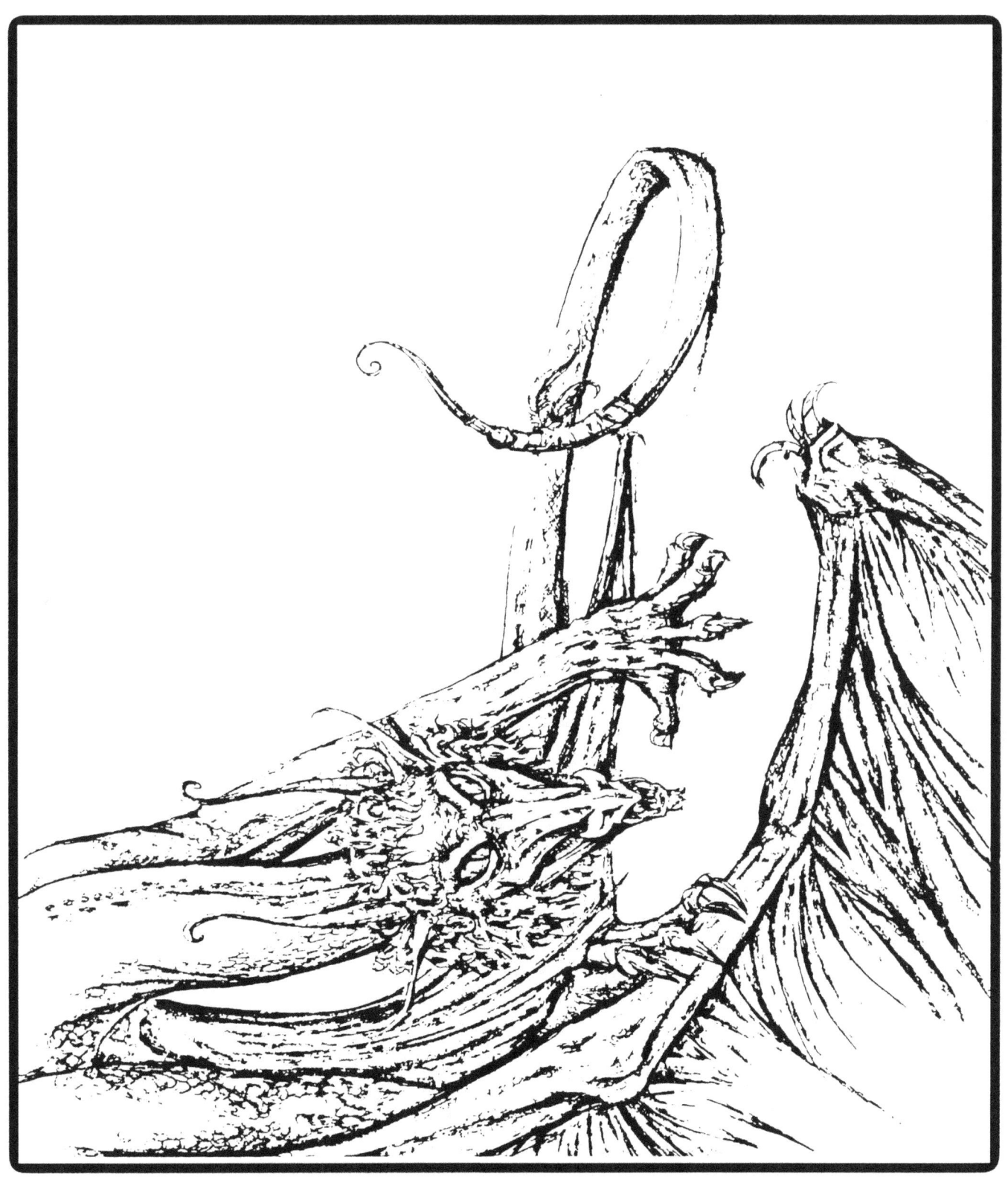

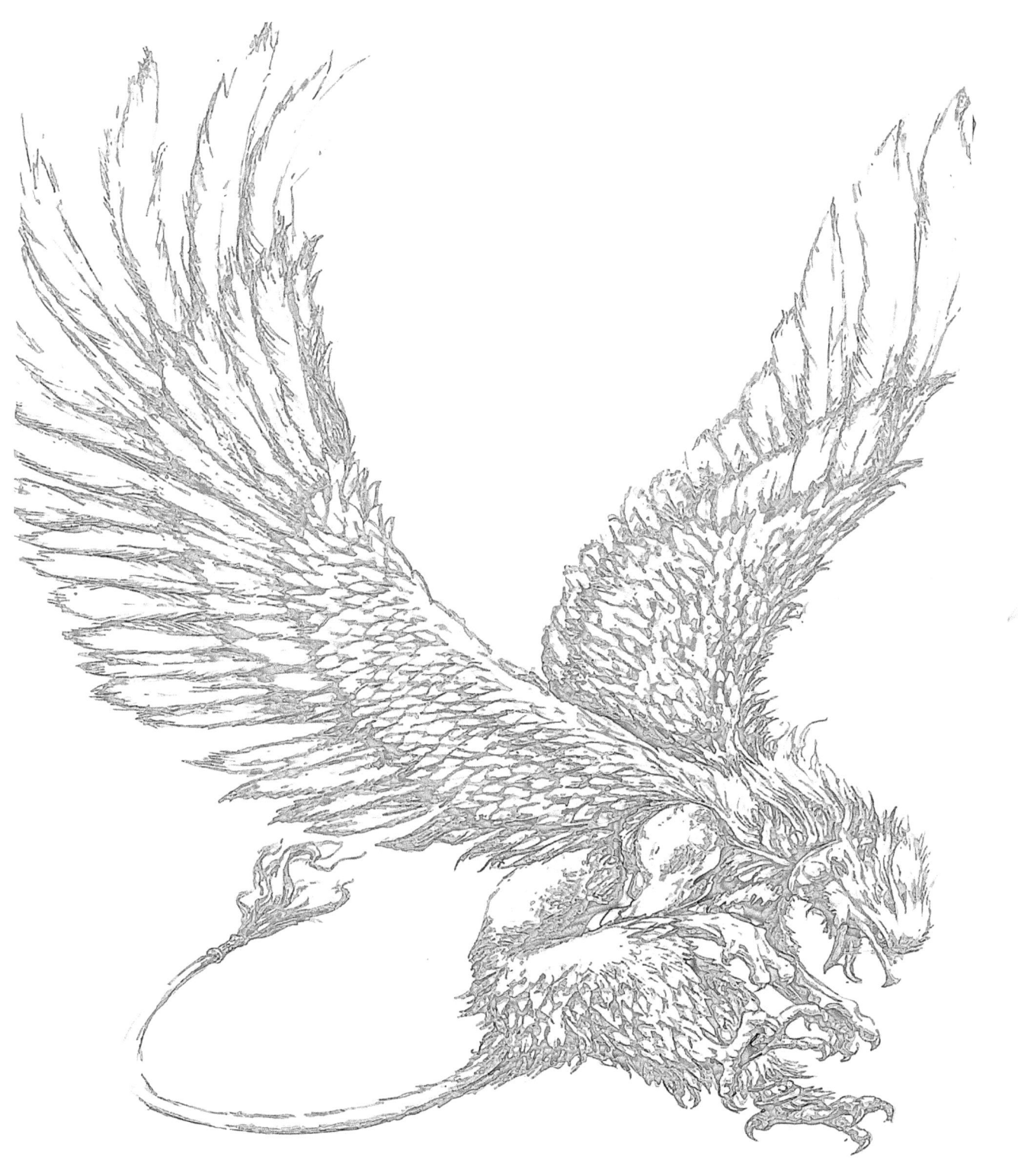

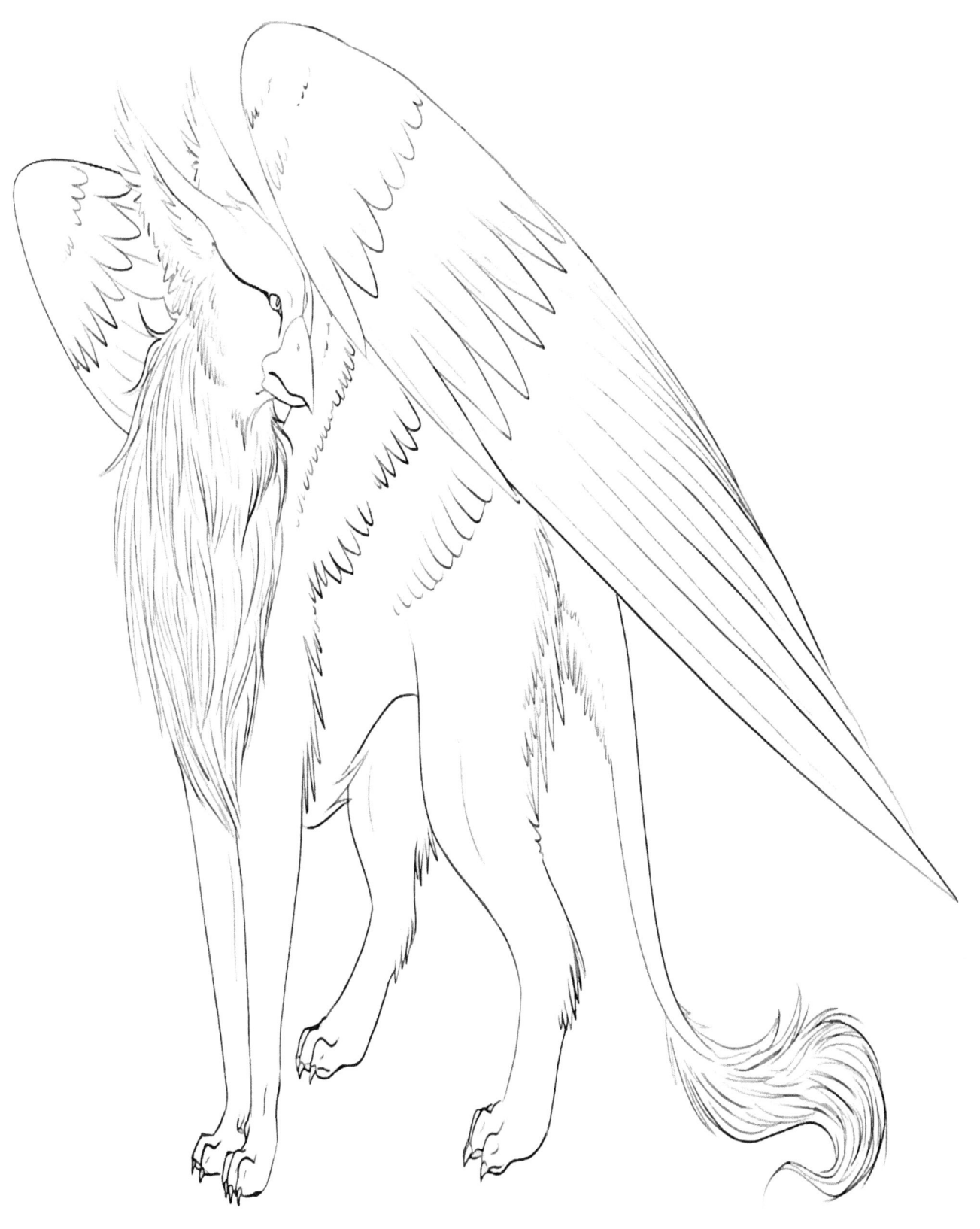

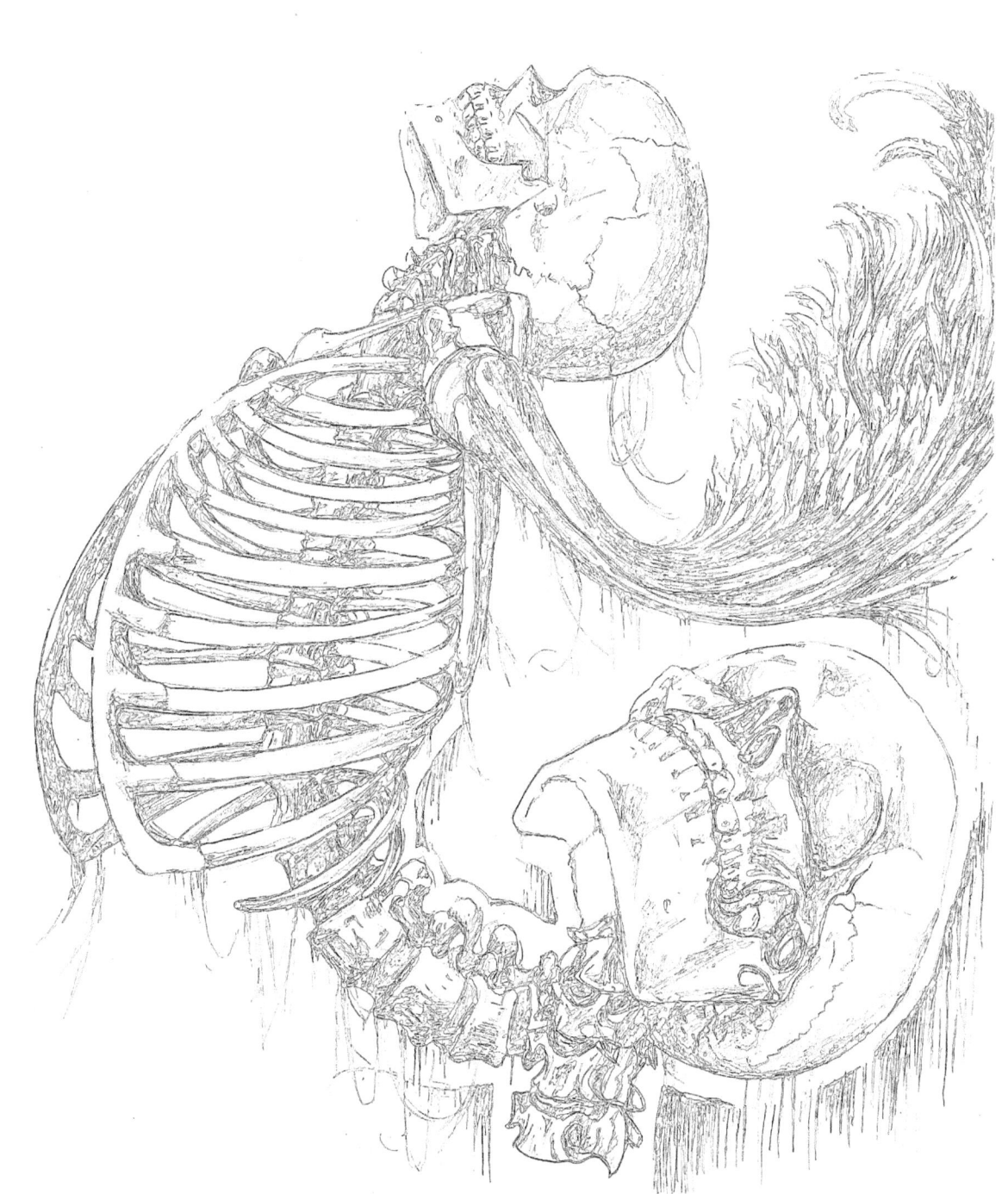

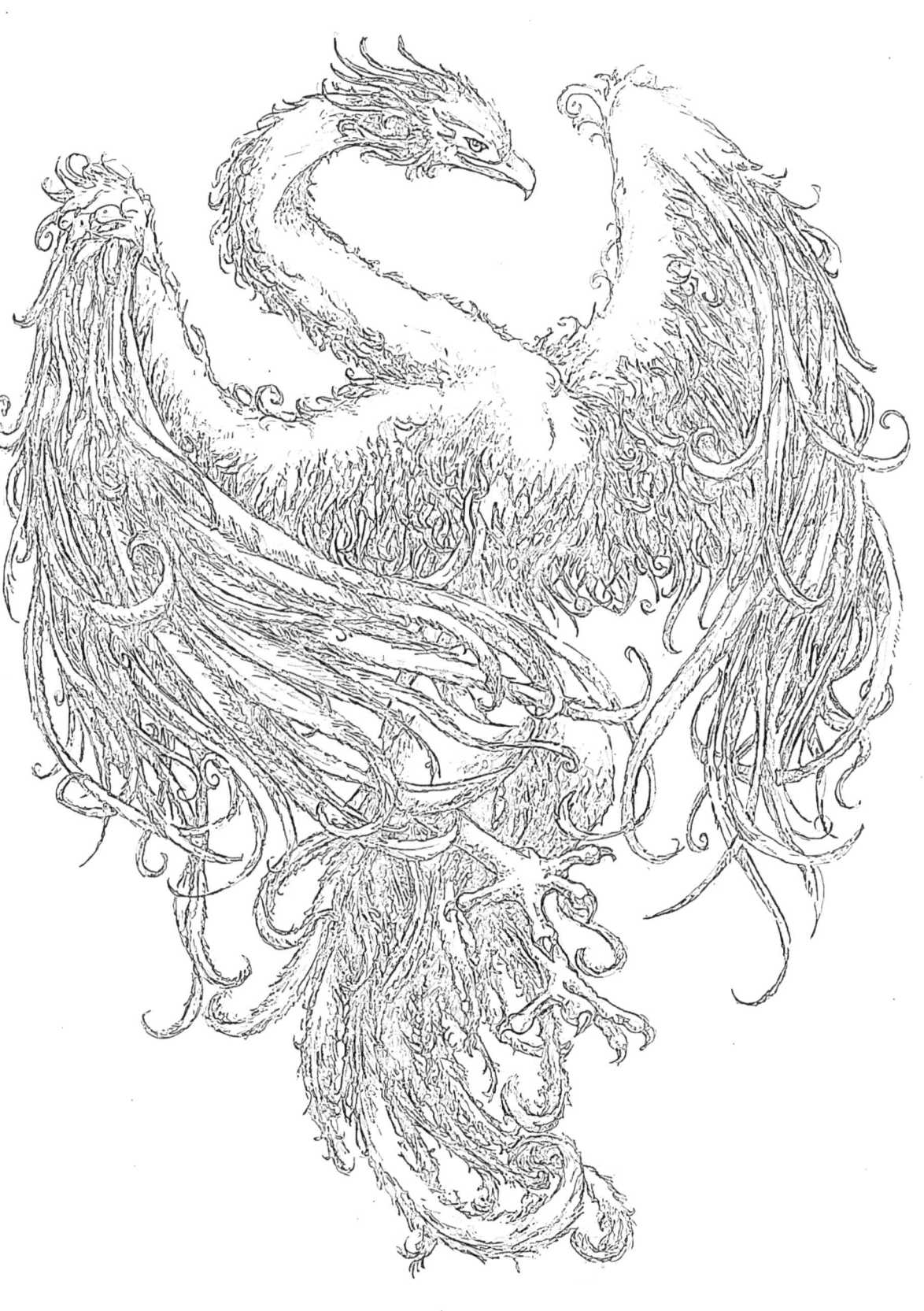

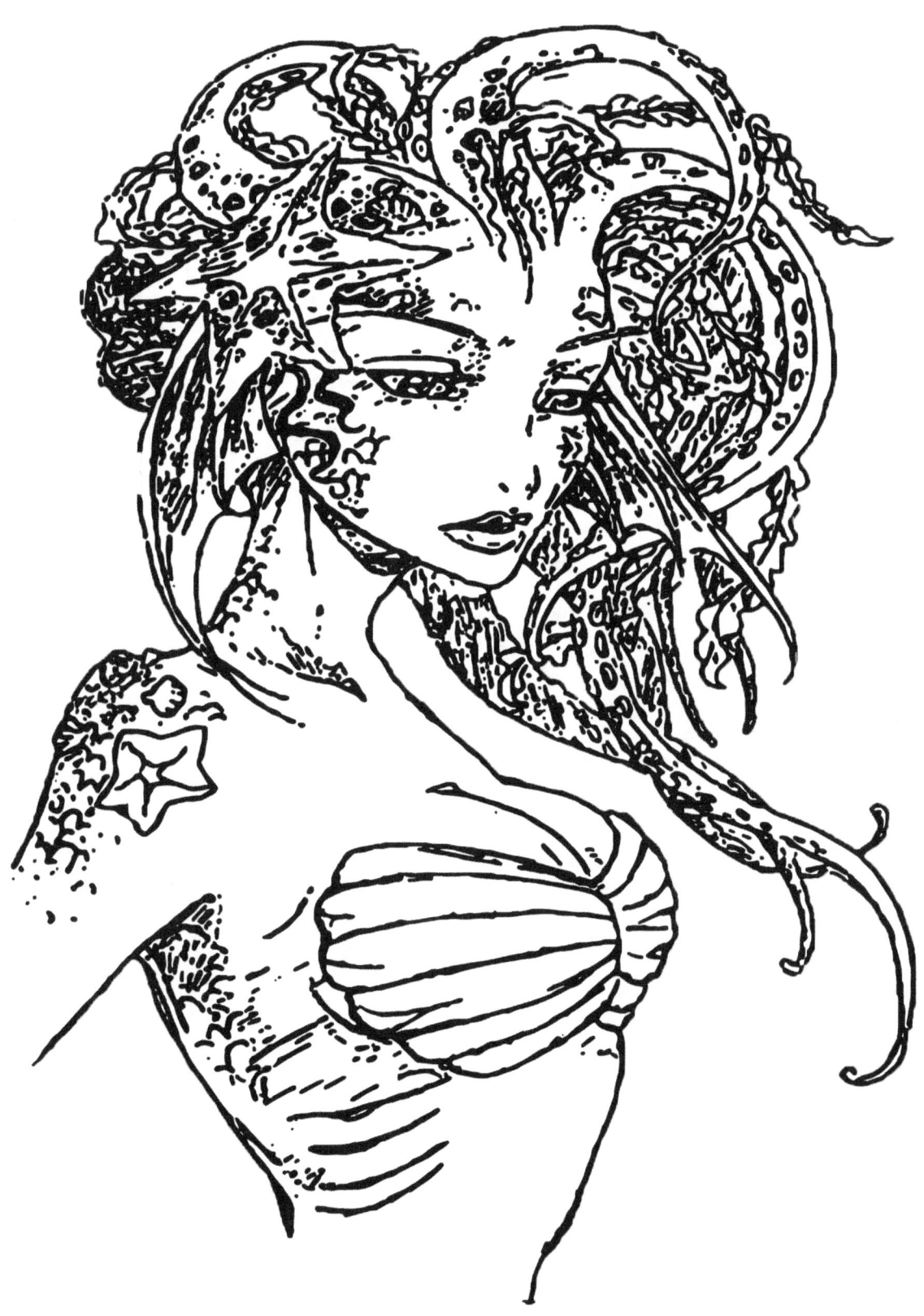

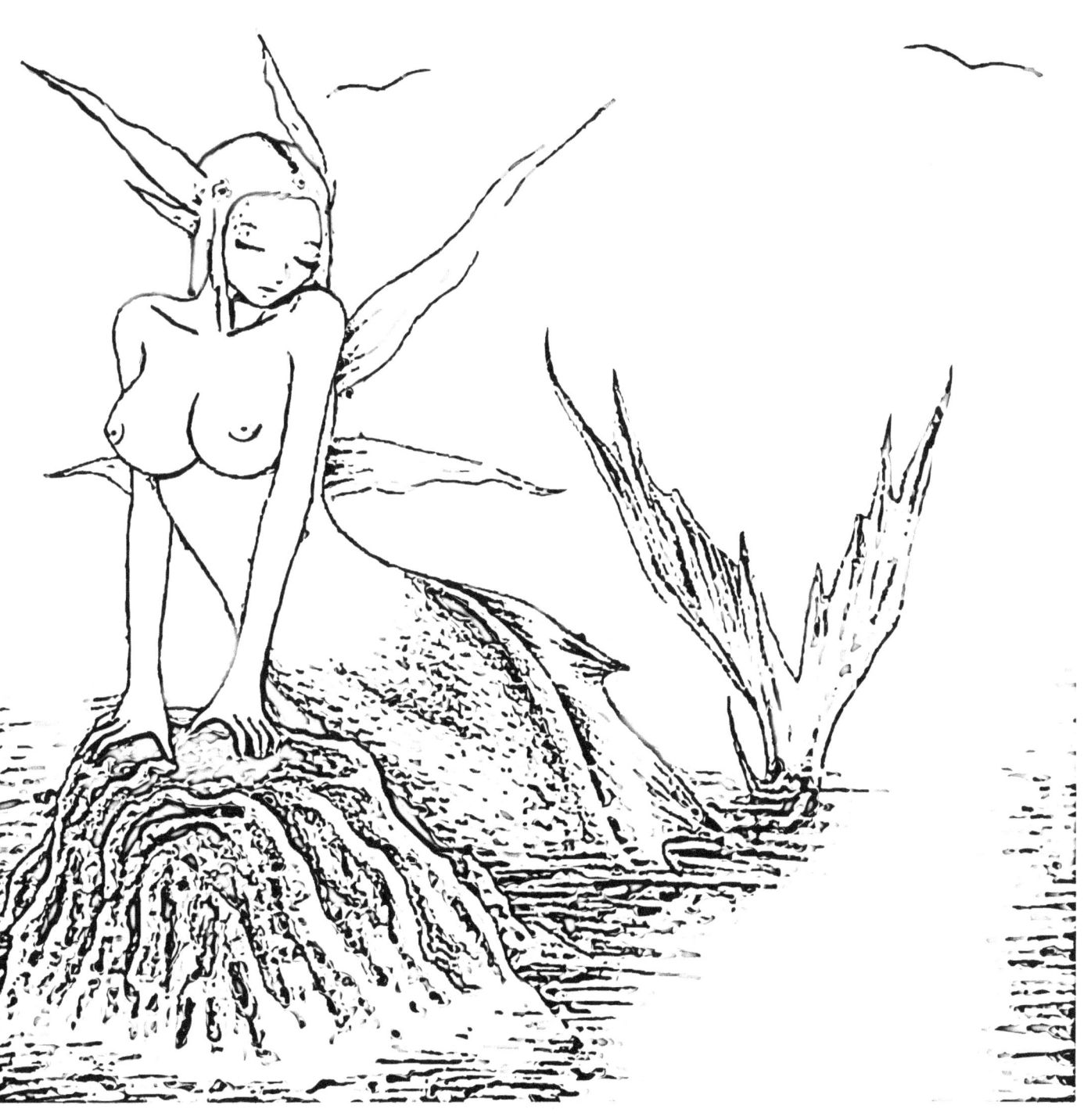